JAMA CA BAY   THE BELT PARKWAY

JAMAICA BAY
THE BELT PARKWAY

STRUCTURES OF COASTAL RESILIENCE

Jamaica Bay Team
Spitzer School of Architecture
The City College of New York

Catherine Seavitt Nordenson, editor
Associate Professor of Landscape Architecture

Kjirsten Alexander
Research Associate

Danae Alessi
Research Associate

Eli Sands
Research Assistant

Fern Lan Siew
Research Assistant

JAMAICA BAY PAMPHLET LIBRARY
03 Jamaica Bay   The Belt Parkway

ISBN 978-1-942900-03-0

CONTACT

Catherine Seavitt Nordenson
cseavittnordenson@ccny.cuny.edu
www.structuresofcoastalresilience.org

SCR Jamaica Bay Team
The City College of New York
Spitzer School of Architecture
Program in Landscape Architecture, Room 2M24A
141 Convent Avenue New York, New York 10031

COVER

Belt Parkway over Spring Creek.
photo: Don Riepe

supported by

   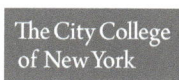

HISTORY

When Robert Moses became Chairman of the State Council of Parks In 1924, New York City was facing transit congestion as growing numbers of automobiles competed with pedestrians, streetcars, elevated trains and horse-drawn freight carts on the city streets.[1] Moses, who was viewed as "a gifted opportunist and pragmatic administrator, able to shepherd public works projects through to completion at a breakneck pace by shrewdly accumulating institutional power and harnessing ever shifting funding streams,"[2] would go on to build a web of parkways, bridges, and expressways into a comprehensive highway network that spanned all five boroughs.

His first public project upon taking office in 1924 was Jones Beach State Park. In order to provide access to this new facility on the south shore of Long Island, he simultaneously began work on a network of parkways that would span the region and connect the public to a recreational network.[3]

Along the route of the Belt Parkway, Moses planned a series of "ribbon parks." These ribbons were composed of playgrounds, promenades, and walkways constructed along the parkway right-of-way. "Moses believed that landscaped, controlled-access parkways would provide for not only efficient traffic flow, but also development of desirable residential growth. Obtaining this land would be easy, since most of it was still undeveloped."[7]

In its 1937 report, "New Parkways in New York City," the New York City Parks Department outlined the Belt Parkway proposal as follows:

The Circumferential Parkway begins at Owl's Head Park at the Narrows, and follows the Shore Drive through Fort Hamilton and Dyker Beach Park. The City of New York was vested title in an extension along Gravesend Bay to Bensonhurst Park, and is about to acquire the remaining rights-of-way up to Guilder Avenue, including sufficient land for the conversion of Guilder Avenue into a genuine parkway with service roads. It is proposed to acquire the rights-of-way for the extension of Guilder Avenue by means of a new parkway parallel to, and north of Emmons Avenue to the Marine Parkway extension, for which land is already

in the possession of the City. It is proposed to carry the Circumferential Parkway from Flatbush Avenue where the Marine Parkway extension ends, along or near Jamaica Bay to a point on Southern Parkway, just east of the Rockaway division of the Long Island Railroad in Queens. It should be noted that work on the conversion of the Sunrise Highway into a genuine parkway is already under way. This will be known as Southern Parkway.

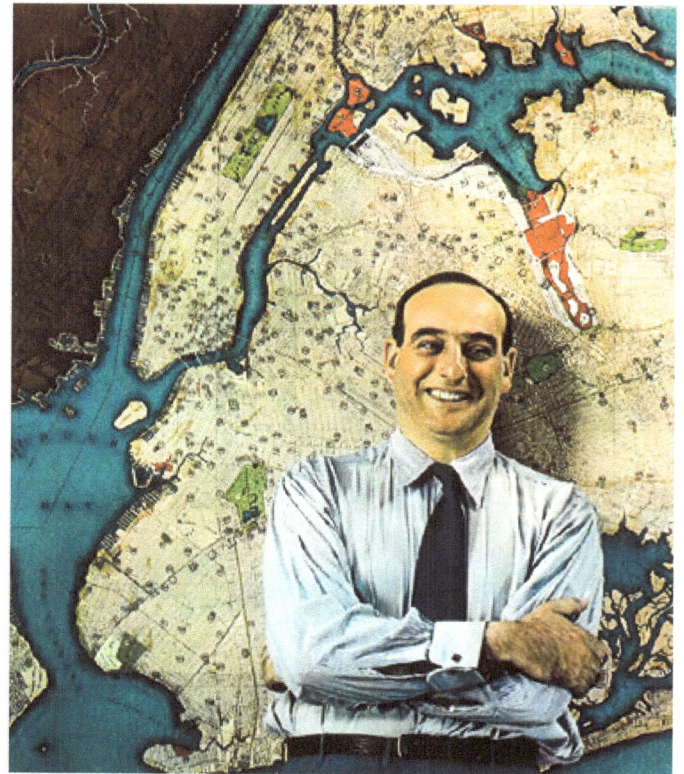

Robert Moses
source: Fortune Magazine, 1938. Photo by Fernand Bourges

1. Gutfreud, p.86
2. Gutfreud, p.93
3. Gutfreud, p.86
4. Gutfreud, p.86
5. Seely, in Gutreud, p.86
6. Gutfreud, p.86
7. Davis and Campanella, in Gutreud, p.87

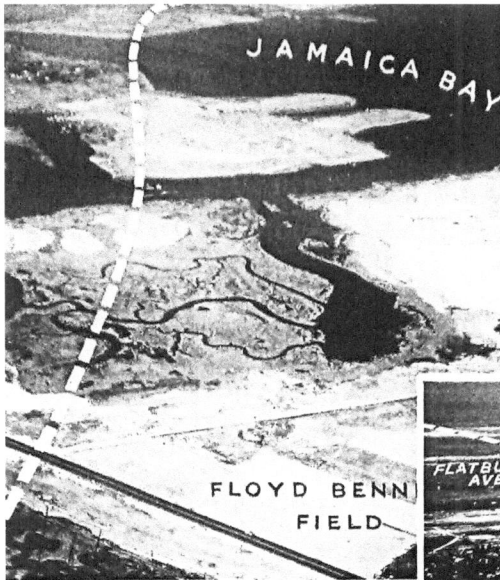

BROOKLYN CIRCUM-FERENTIAL PARKWAY

← Leaving Southern Park-way the Circumferential Parkway crosses the meadow land in a southwesterly direction, and skirts the shore of Jamaica Bay in front of Canarsie Beach Park;—

it crosses Flatbush Avenue just north of Floyd Bennett Field and passes thru Marine Park north of Plumb Island;—

←. then it parallels Emmons, Guider, and Cropsey Avenues to Bensonhurst Park.

Proposed route along the shore of Jamaica Bay, from The Belt Parkway, 1940
source: New York City Department of Parks and Recreation Arsenal Library

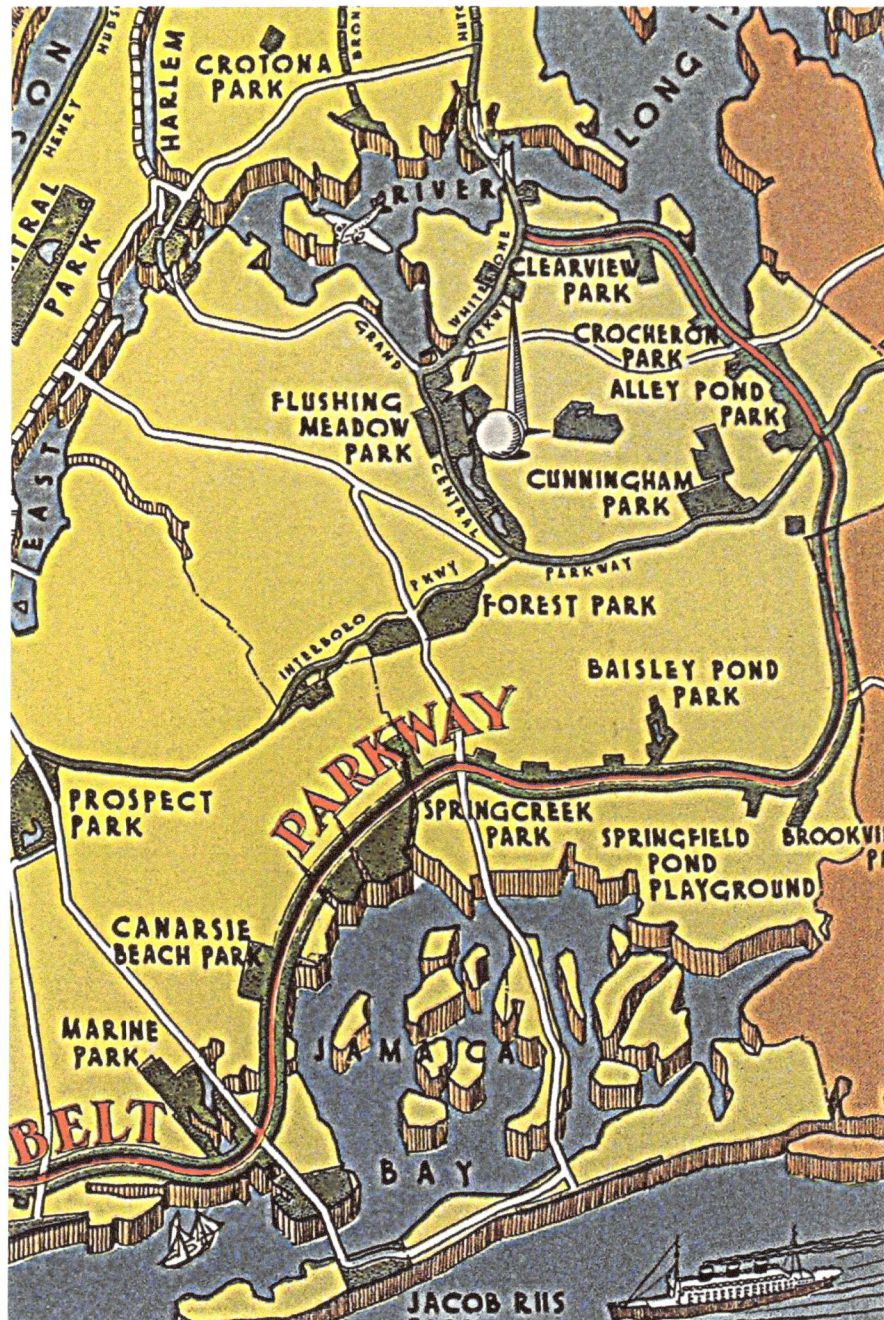

Map from Opening the Belt Parkway, a promotional booklet for the proposed parkway, 1940
source: New York City Department of Parks and Recreation Arsenal Library

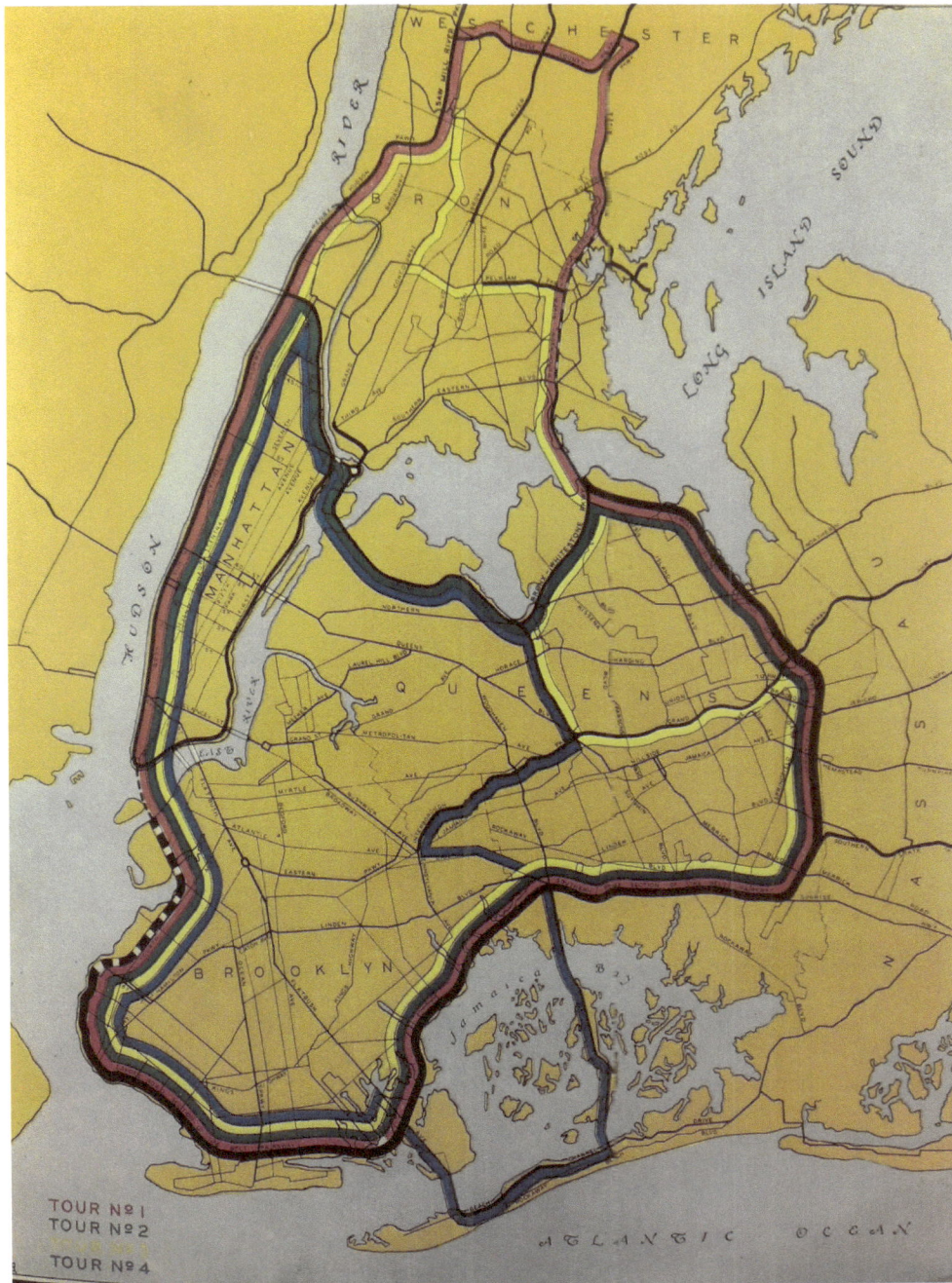

Robert Moses' suggested touring roads along the Belt System, from The Belt Parkway, 1940
source: New York City Department of Parks and Recreation Arsenal Library

Belt Parkway under construction near Marine Park, 1939
source: New York City Parks Photo Archive

Belt Parkway under construction, 1941
source: New York City Parks Photo Archive

OPENING

The opening of the Belt Parkway in 1941 was met with much fanfare. The new system linked 26 major new parks totaling over 3,550 acres of City land, making the Belt Parkway System the largest city park in New York City. The public was encouraged to use it so that the purposes that Moses and the Regional Plan Association had outlined for it could be achieved. It was meant to relieve traffic congestion and create a system by which people could easily access recreational activities. The Parkway itself was to function as a leisurely driving road that offered scenic tours of the city.

After opening, the Parkway was still missing two stretches: the extension in the Brooklyn-Battery Tunnel and the short section in Sheepshead Bay, parallel to Emmons Avenue. The Emmons Avenue link was opened a year later, despite much opposition from the local residents who were upset by the demolition that had been necessary to create the Parkway. This expansion included new recreational park elements along Emmons and Cropsey Avenues. This was one of the few recorded times that monetary awards were given as compensation to displaced private citizens during the creation of new transportation infrastructure.

By 1944 the Shore Parkway was slated for an additional lane expansion, but World War II and a lack of funds prevented the project from moving forward. Two years later, the project was begun, and the Shore Parkway's expansion from two lanes to three was completed by 1947. In 1949, Moses continued the expansion by adding a third lane to the Southern and Cross Island parkways. While appearing minimal, these expansions overtook 106 acres of a planted median strip.

SOURCES

Owen D. Getfreud, "Rebuilding New York in the Auto Age: Robert Moses and his Highways," in Robert Moses and the Modern City: The Transformation of New York. Ballon, H., & Jackson, K. T., eds. New York, NY: W.W. Norton & Co., 2007.

The Belt Parkway. New York, NY: New York City Department of Parks and Recreation, July 1, 1940.

Caro, R. A. The Power Broker: Robert Moses and the Fall of New York. New York, NY: Knopf, 1974.

BIKEWAY

The Belt Parkway Bikeway was part of Moses' original design, hugging Brooklyn's shoreline for thirteen miles. The bikeway is composed of three sections between Exit 1 (65th Street-67th Street) in Bay Ridge and Exit 5 (Bay Parkway) in Gravesend. There are gaps between Bay Parkway and Knapp Street in Sheepzshead Bay with the next section starting at Cross Bay Boulevard in Howard Beach. New York City plans to close the gap in the bikeway, and upgrade it between Knapp Street and Cross Bay Boulevard.

The Belt Parkway Bikeway connects with the Rockaway Greenway, providing access to the Rockaway beaches, Jamaica Bay Wildlife Refuge, and Floyd Bennett Field. The current proposed system for the Belt Parkway Bikeway is to link the bikeway as a spur of the East Coast Greenway and to improve the bikeway's links with the local street network.

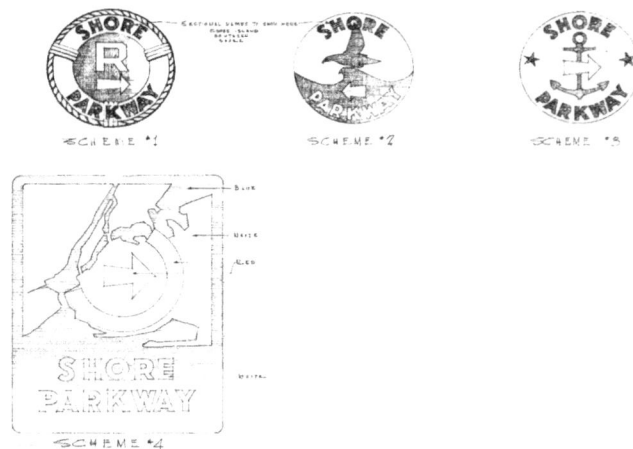

Sketch and Proposed Route Markers and Symbols, 1940
source: Courtesy The City of New York, Department of Parks and Recreation, Map File

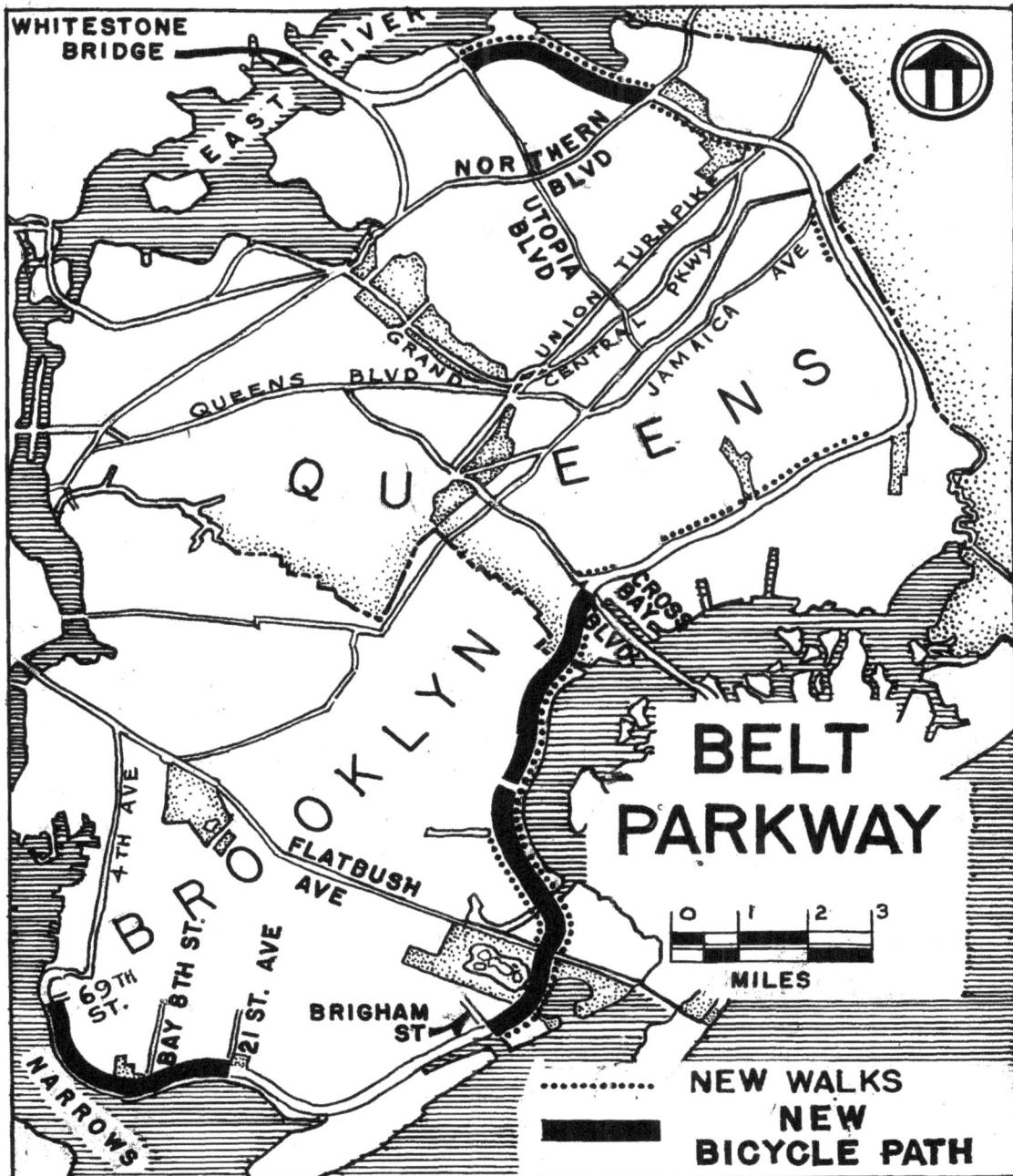

Map of proposed bicycle path for the Belt Parkway, 1941
source: Courtesy The City of New York, Department of Parks and Recreation, Map File

FACTS

- 11.8 million cubic yards of hydraulic fill pumped

- 4.8 million cubic yards of dry fill moved

- 1.5 million square yards of pavement used

- 530,000 cubic yards of concrete used

- 11,500 cubic yards of masonry used

- 400,000 linear feet of piles used

- 320,000 tons of steel used

- 9,000 men employed

source: www.nycroads.com

Four teens bike the path along the Belt Parkway
source: New York City Parks Photo Archive. Photo by Rodney McCay Morgan

Clearview Beach

Clearview Park Golf Course

Crocheron Park

Cross Island Parkway

Alley Pond Park

Grand Central Parkway

Pat Williams Playground

Laurelton Parkway

Baisley Pond Park

Laurelton Playground

Belt Parkway

Brookville Park

Southern Fields

Spring Creek Park

Leif Ericson Drive

Fresh Creek Nature Preserve

Shore Road Park and Parkway

Canarsie Park

Ocean Parkway Malls

Paerdegat Basin Park

McGuire Fields

Dyker Beach Park

Bath Beach Park

Marine Park

Four Sparrow Marsh

Bensonhurst Park

Calvert Vaux Park

Grady Playground

0   1.25   2.5   5 Miles

NEW YORK CITY PARKS ADJACENT TO PARKWAYS

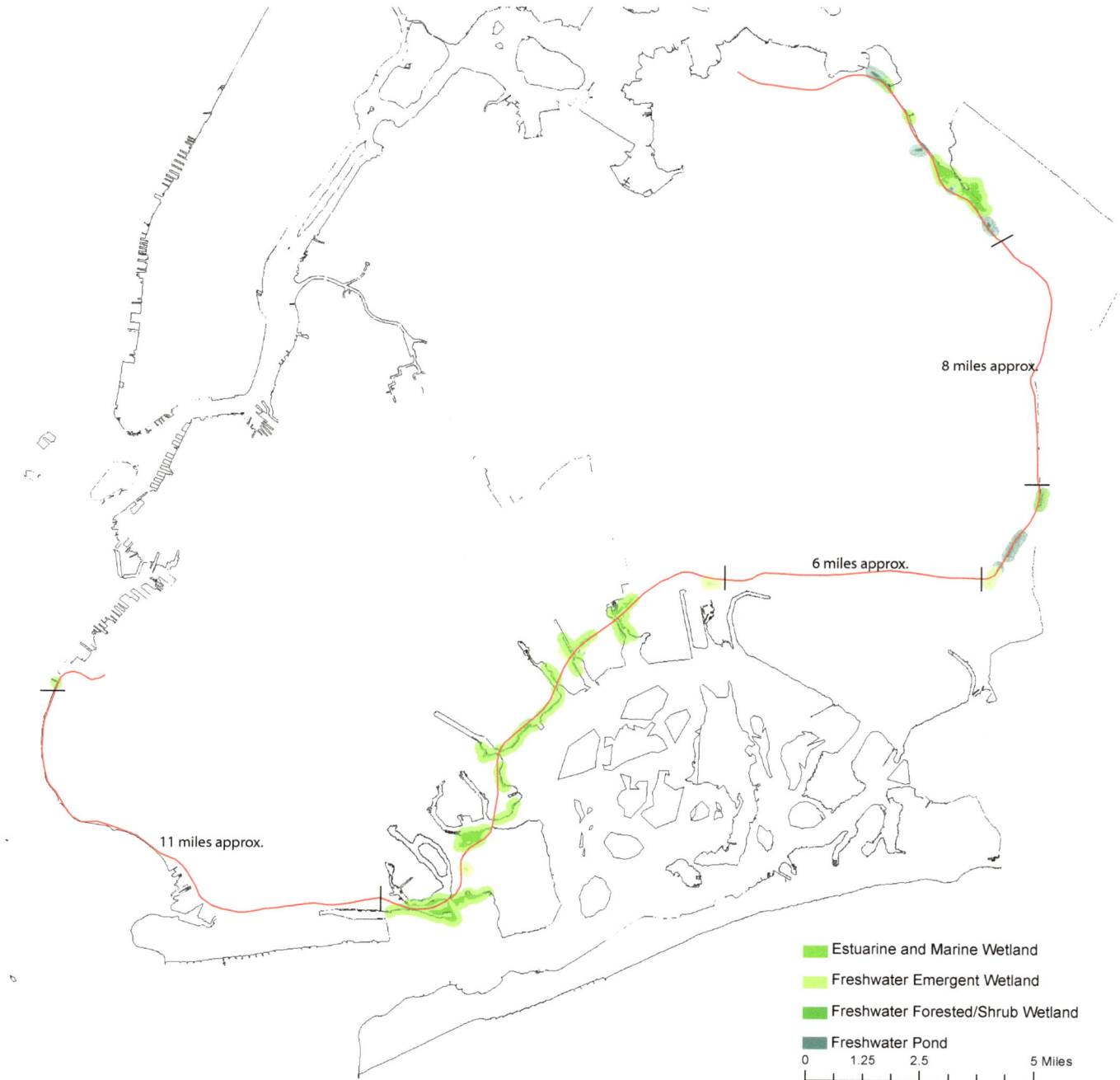

8 miles approx.

6 miles approx.

11 miles approx.

Estuarine and Marine Wetland

Freshwater Emergent Wetland

Freshwater Forested/Shrub Wetland

Freshwater Pond

0   1.25   2.5   5 Miles

WETLANDS

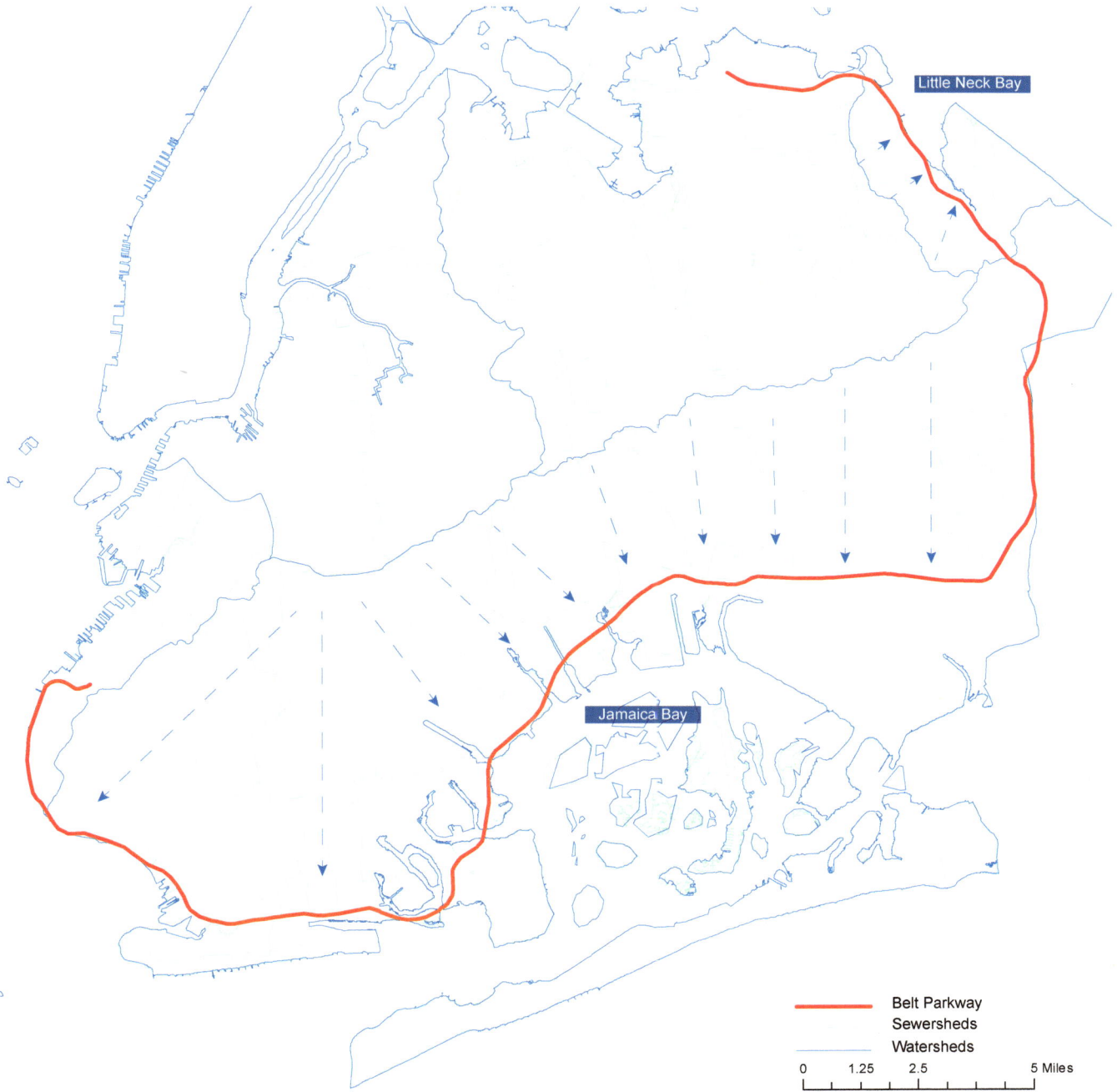

Little Neck Bay

Jamaica Bay

Belt Parkway
Sewersheds
Watersheds

0   1.25   2.5   5 Miles

WATERSHEDS AND SEWERSHEDS

OWNERSHIP

Our search for opportunities led us to examine the ownership of the Belt Parkway. This question is not easily answered. While originally under clear ownership of the New York City Parks Department, over time this status became somewhat murky because the Parkway has operated more like a highway than a shoestring park. Some indication as to who owns the fifty acres of vegetated grassy medians, trees, and verges along the Belt Parkway seems to come from a ruling that was handed down in 2002. That year, the NYC Law Department ruled that a "4F" statement should be in effect for areas of the Belt Parkway for areas adjacent to the Belt Parkway.

A "4F" is an environmental signoff, guaranteeing that there would be no impact on parkland from proposed work by the Department of Transportation on the Belt Parkway. The Law Department reasoned that the landscaped areas within the right-of-way of the Belt Parkway were not technically considered "park." The Parks Department now acts only in an advisory capacity to the DOT in order to ensure that major infrastructural improvements have minimal environmental impacts.

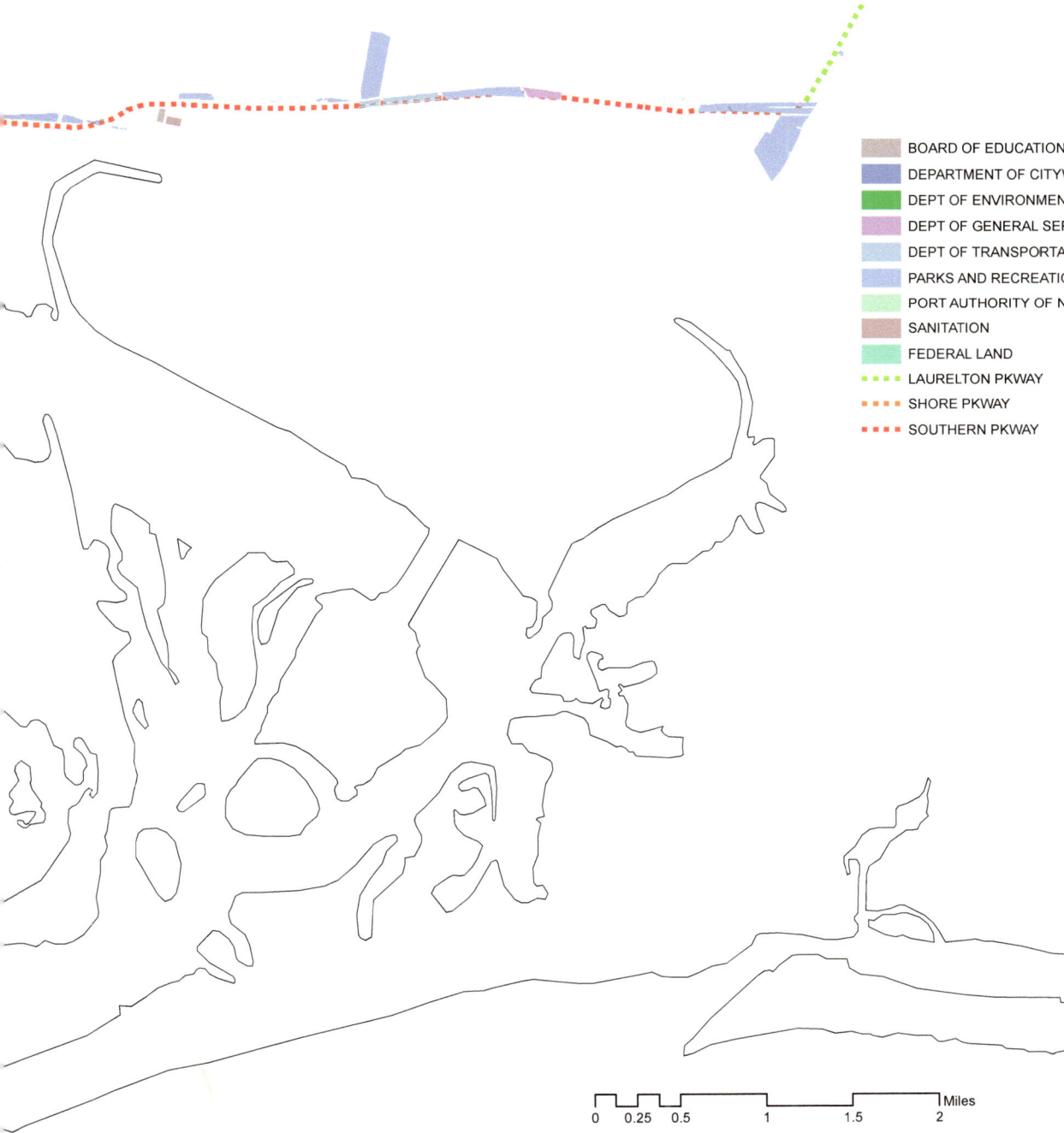

BOARD OF EDUCATION
DEPARTMENT OF CITYWIDE ADMINISTRATIVE SERVICES
DEPT OF ENVIRONMENTAL PROTECTION
DEPT OF GENERAL SERVICES
DEPT OF TRANSPORTATION
PARKS AND RECREATION
PORT AUTHORITY OF NY
SANITATION
FEDERAL LAND
LAURELTON PKWAY
SHORE PKWAY
SOUTHERN PKWAY

Miles
0   0.25   0.5   1   1.5   2

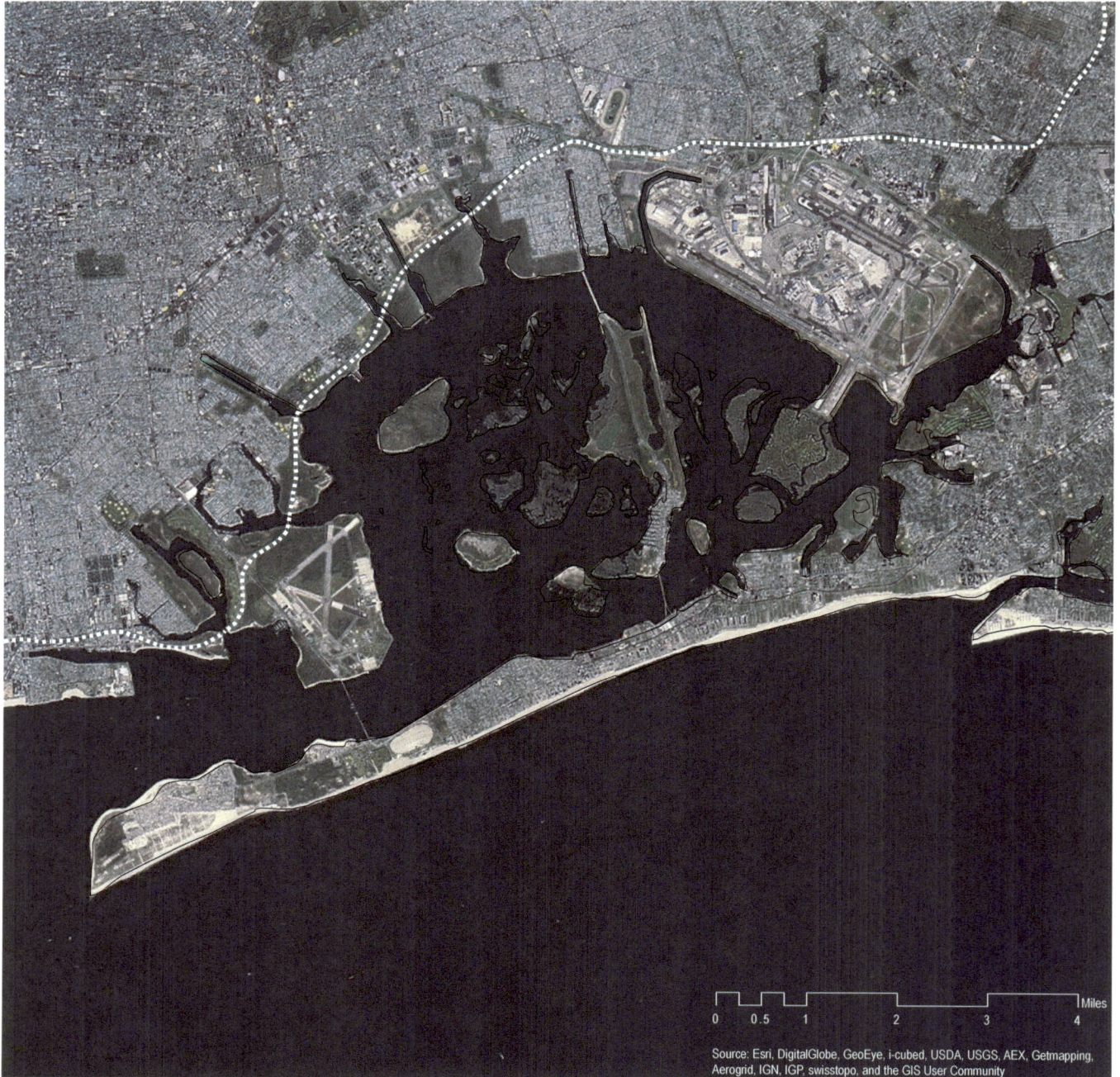

Source: Esri, DigitalGlobe, GeoEye, i-cubed, USDA, USGS, AEX, Getmapping, Aerogrid, IGN, IGP, swisstopo, and the GIS User Community

AERIAL IMAGE

SPRING CREEK

FRESH CREEK BASIN

HENDRIX CREEK

ROCKAWAY PARKWAY

PAERDEGAT BASIN

MILL BASIN

GERRITSEN INLET

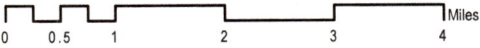

Miles

0   0.5   1   2   3   4

BRIDGES

GERRITSEN INLET

0   150 300   600   900   1,200 Feet

SPAN: **464'**

ELEVATION: **42.75'**
above Brooklyn Highway Datum (MSL + 2.56')

YEAR CONSTRUCTED: **1938**

source: NYC DOT

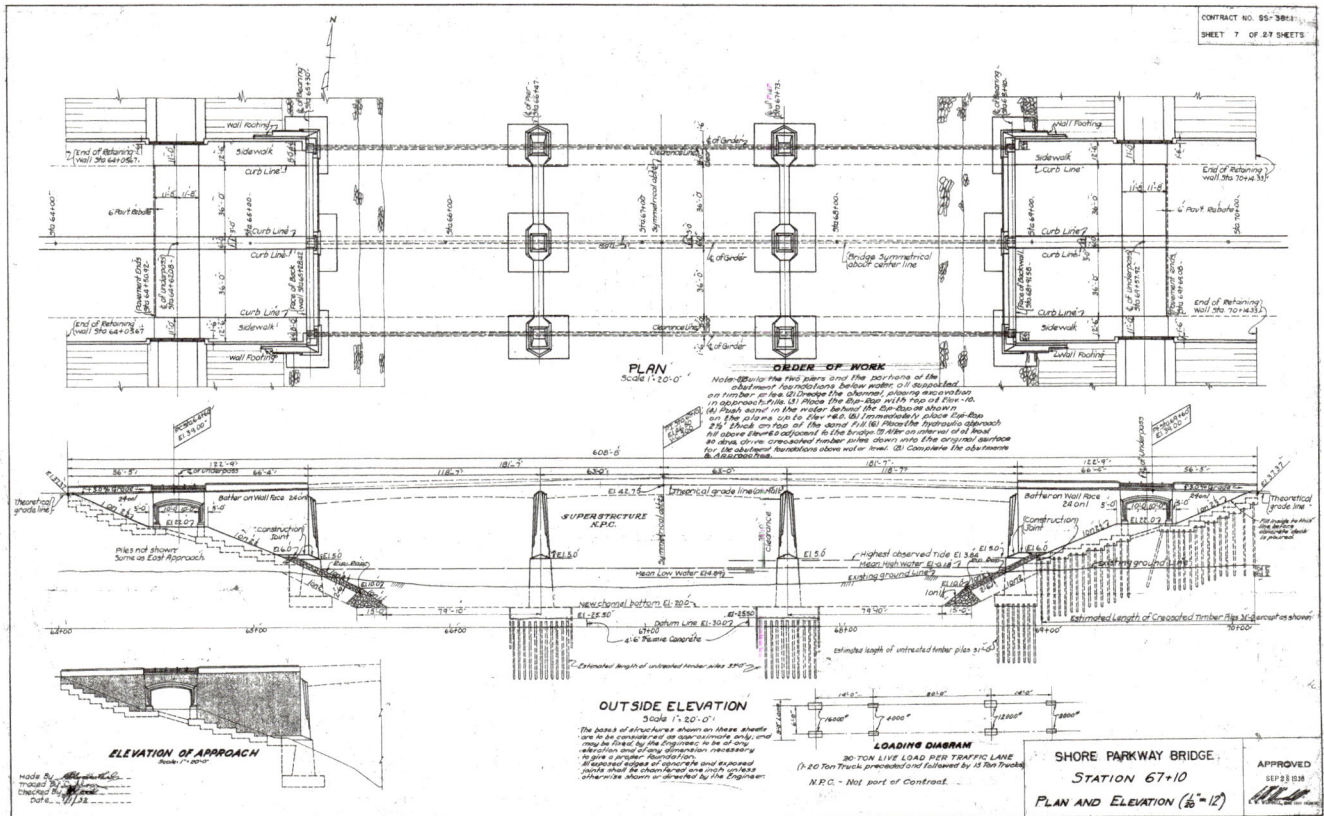

Shore Parkway Bridge at Gerritsen Inlet, Plan and Elevation
source: Courtesy The City of New York, Department of Parks and Recreation, Map File

MILL BASIN

Feet
0 150 300   600   900   1,200

SPAN: **744'**

ELEVATION: **49'**
above Brooklyn Highway Datum (MSL + 2.56')

YEAR CONSTRUCTED: **1939**

source: NYC DOT

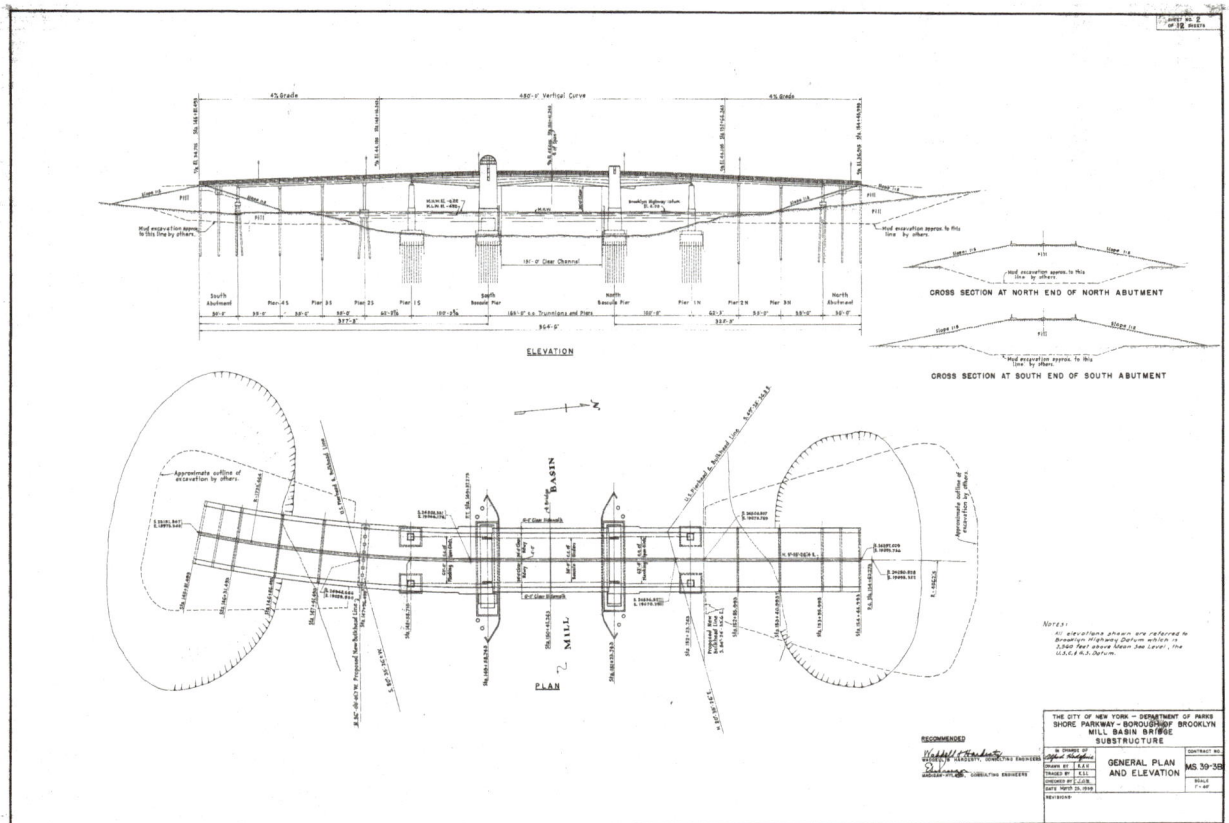

Shore Parkway, Mill Basin Bridge Substructure, General Plan and Elevation
source: Courtesy The City of New York, Department of Parks and Recreation, Map File

PAERDEGAT BASIN

SPAN:	**701'**
ELEVATION:	**34.5'**
above Brooklyn Highway Datum (MSL + 2.56')	
YEAR CONSTRUCTED:	**1939**
RECONSTRUCTED:	**2013**

source: NYC DOT

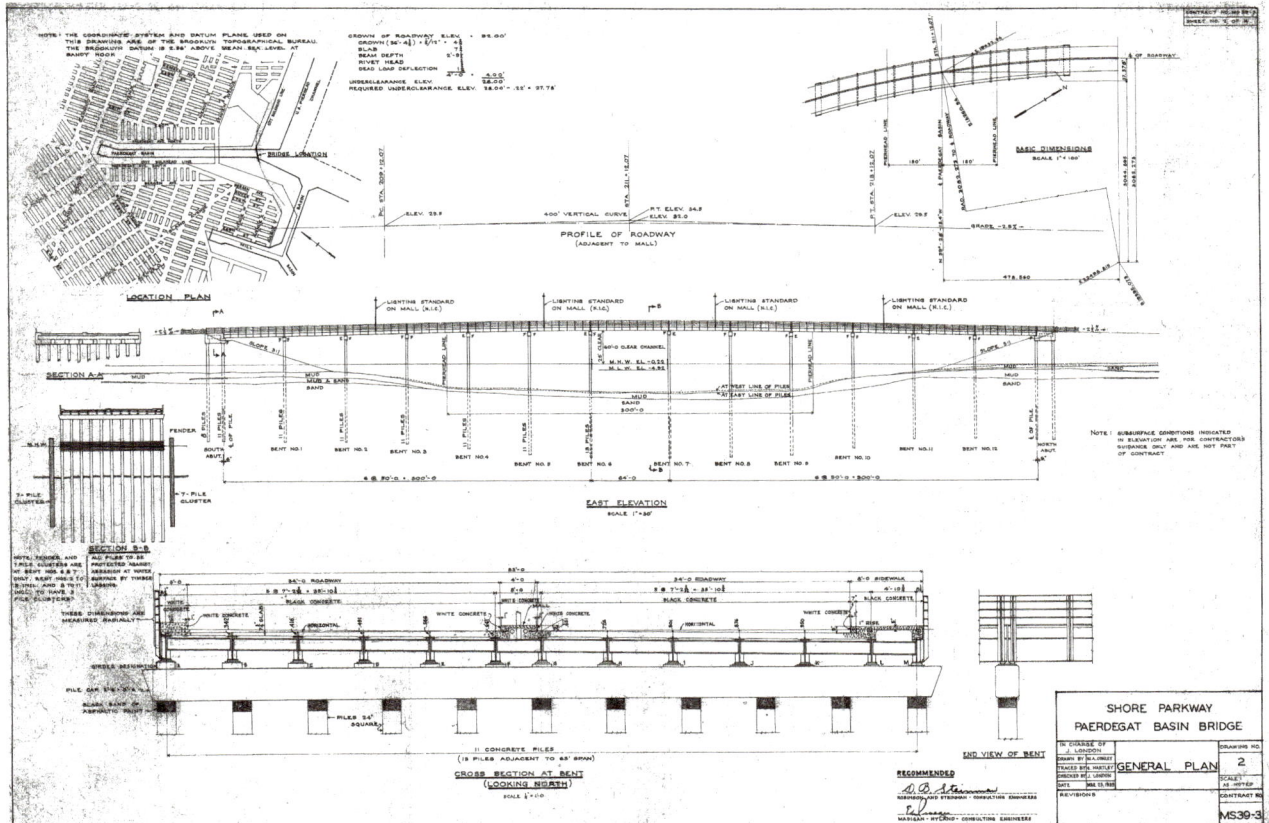

Shore Parkway, Paerdegat Basin Bridge, General Plan
source: Courtesy The City of New York, Department of Parks and Recreation, Map File

ROCKAWAY PARKWAY

0   150 300   600   900   1,200 Feet

SPAN: 153'

ELEVATION: 26'
above Brooklyn Highway Datum (MSL + 2.56')

YEAR CONSTRUCTED: 1938

source: NYC DOT

Shore Parkway, Grade Separation at Rockaway Parkway, General Plan and Profiles
source: Courtesy The City of New York, Department of Parks and Recreation, Map File

FRESH CREEK

SPAN: **401'**

ELEVATION: **28'**
above Brooklyn Highway Datum (MSL + 2.56')

YEAR CONSTRUCTED: **1939**

RECONSTRUCTED: **2013**

source: NYC DOT

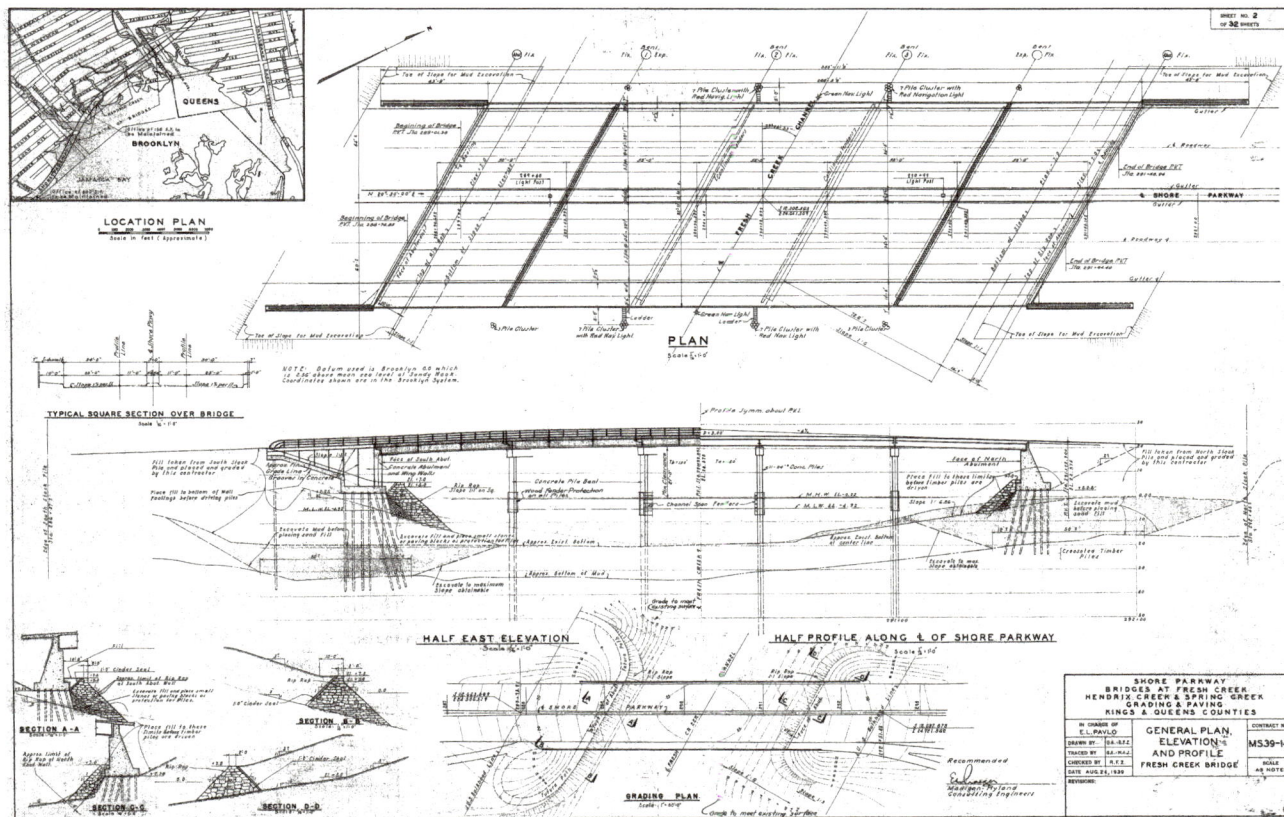

Shore Parkway, General Plan, Elevation, and Profile at Fresh Creek Bridge
source: Courtesy The City of New York, Department of Parks and Recreation, Map File

HENDRIX CREEK

SPAN: 271'

ELEVATION: 25'
above Brooklyn Highway Datum (MSL + 2.56')

YEAR CONSTRUCTED: 1938

source: www.flickr.com/photos/jag9889/5915517237/

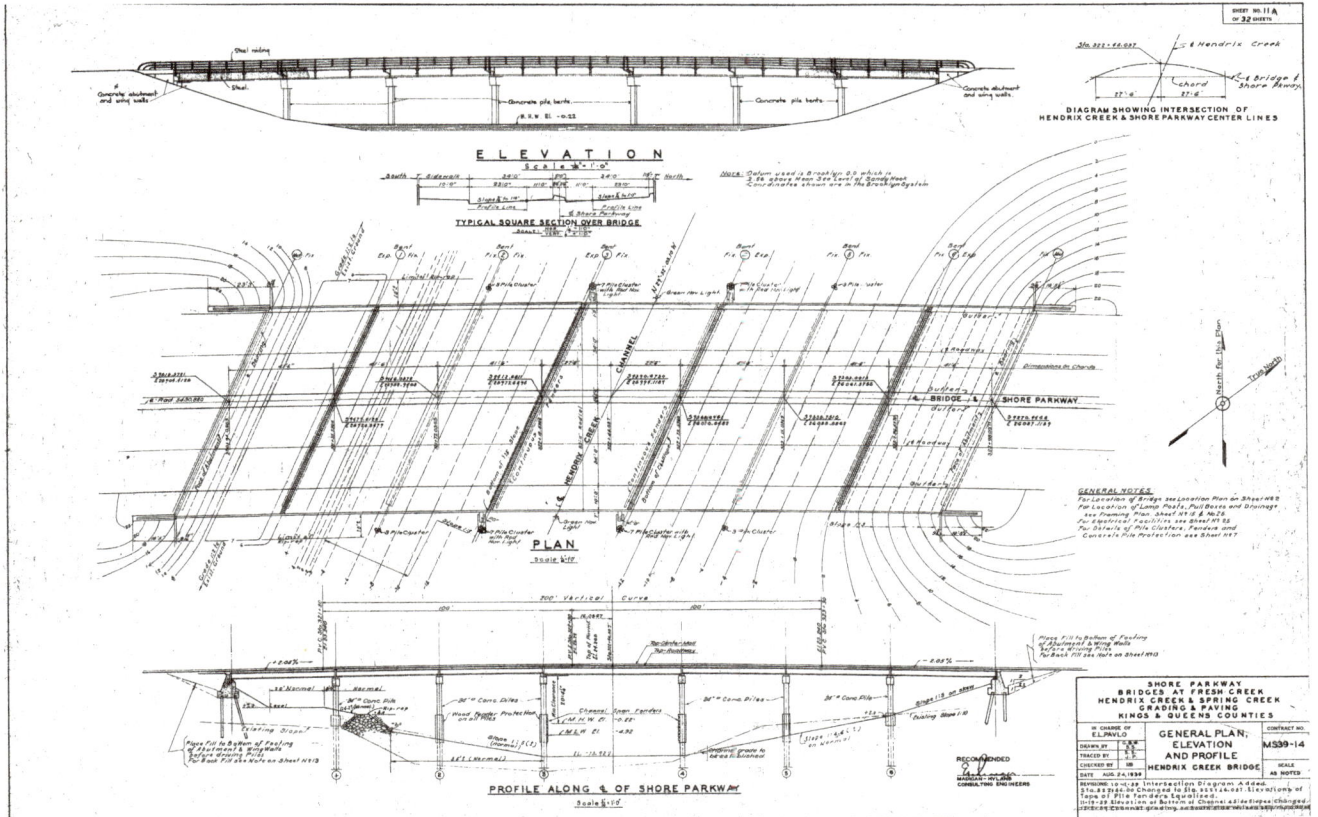

Shore Parkway, General Plan, Elevation, and Profile at Hendrix Creek Bridge
source: Courtesy The City of New York, Department of Parks and Recreation, Map File

SPRING CREEK

0   150 300   600   900   1,200   Feet

SPAN: 312'

ELEVATION: 29'
above Brooklyn Highway Datum (MSL + 2.56')

YEAR CONSTRUCTED: 1939

source: longdistancevoyager.blogspot.com/2011/07/bridge-of-week-63-spring-creek-bbridge.html

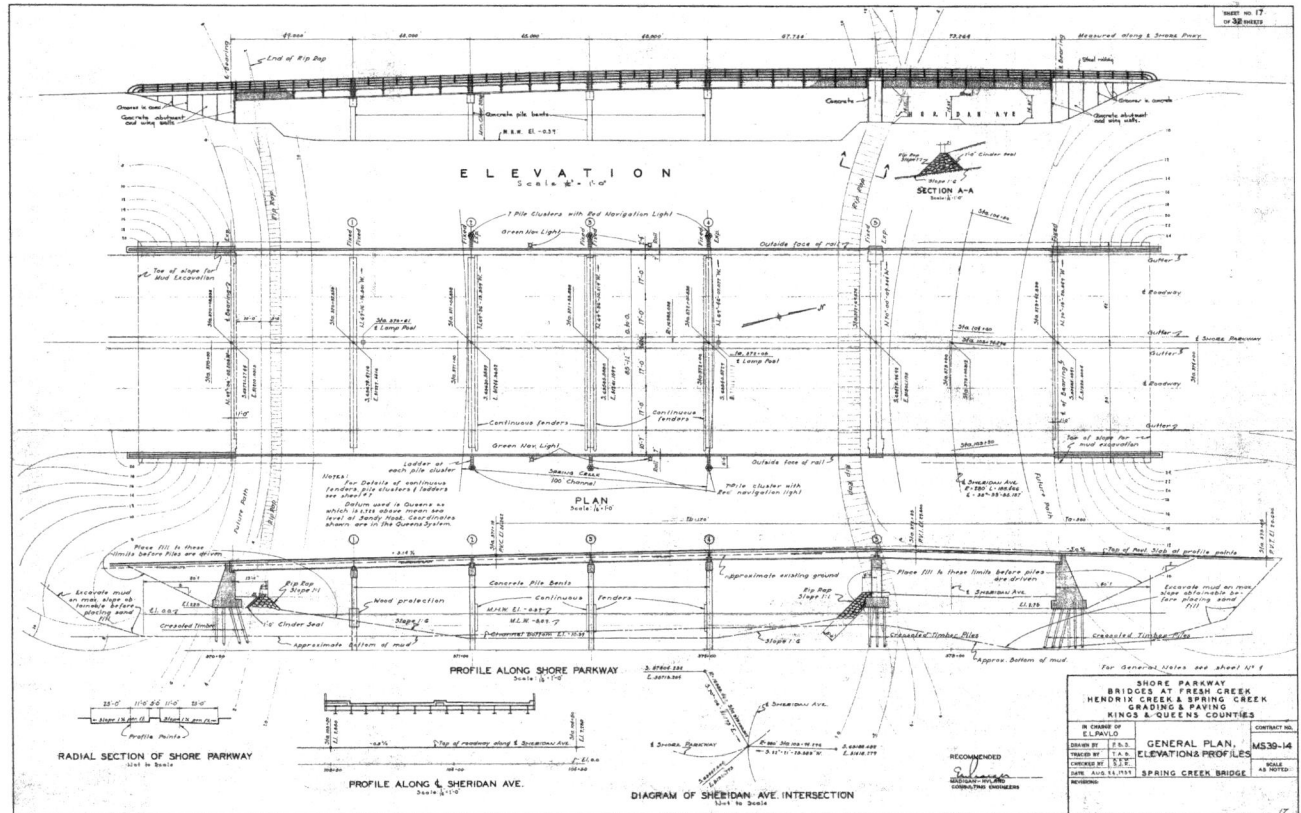

Shore Parkway, General Plan, Elevation, and Profile at Spring Creek Bridge
source: Courtesy The City of New York, Department of Parks and Recreation, Map File

EXIT 11S

Flatbush Ave SOUTH
Rockaways
1/4 MILE

EXIT 11N

Flatbush Ave NORTH
Marine Park

12-4

1/4 MILE

T91·BSY

Gateway National
Recreation Area
Floyd Bennett Field
Riis Park
EXIT 11S

Golf·Tennis / Marina

Sports and Events Center

www.ingramcontent.com/pod-product-compliance
Lightning Source LLC
Chambersburg PA
CBHW060826270326
41931CB00002B/75